Calling All Girls

Calling All book series
Volume 1 Girls

by: Rebecca Joyce Baker

Copyright © 2009 by Rebecca Joyce Baker.
Graphic Artist: Teresa Hobson
Illustrated Graphics by: Othoniel Ortiz
    email:otoenail@yahoo.com
    contact: (734) 818-6895
Designed by: An Angels Touch! LLC

ISBN:	Hardcover	978-1-4257-8526-0
	Softcover	978-1-4257-2358-3

All rights reserved. No part of this book may be reproduced or transmitted in any form or by any means, electronic or mechanical, including photocopying, recording, or by any information storage and retrieval system, without permission in writing from the copyright owner.

Unless otherwise indicated, all scripture quotations are taken from the Holy Bible King James Version/ Amplified Parallel. Copyright 1995 by Zondervan

Teen Info: American College of Obstetricians and Gynecologist. Your First Ob-Gyn Visit. ACOG Patient Education Pamphlet AP150. Washington, D.C: ACOG, 2001.

Printed in the United States of America.

To order additional copies of this book, contact:
Xlibris Corporation
1-888-795-4274
www.Xlibris.com
Orders@Xlibris.com
29201

Presented to a Special Girl

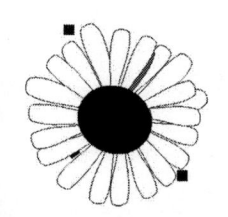

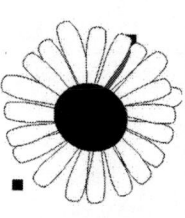

_____

CONTENTS

Dedication 7
Foreword 8
Acknowledgments 9
Introduction 13

Part 1: Exploring to Know Your Body 15
- Female Anatomy Development
- Becoming familiar with me

Part 2: Understanding Puberty—Knowledge is Power 31
- Puberty
- Understanding Menstruation
- Helpful Hints and Practices
- Girl Essentials

Part 3: Teen Info 47
- Your First Visit to the OB/GYN (female specialist doctor)

Part 4: Exploring Personal Hygeine 53
- Personal Cleansing Habits
- Hair Grooming

Part 5: Girl Talk 63
- Distractions

Part 6: Begin Your Day with a daily Prayer . . .
   God loves to hear "your" voice when "you" PRAY!.................... 71
   • Recommended prayers to start your day

Part 7: Motivation 81
   • Scriptures to guide you

Part 8: Did you know?... 91
   • The Origin of Life
   • Created by Design
   • God Created Our Bodies to Live and Walk on Planet Earth
   • Designed for Purpose

Calling All Girls Creed 106

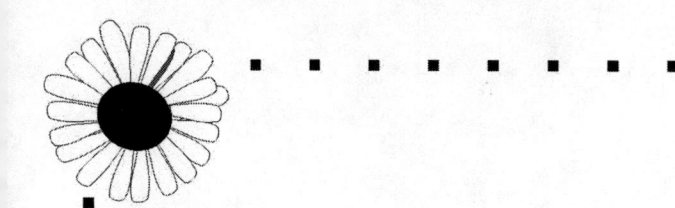

Dedication

I dedicate this book to every daughter of the world
and to my four precious granddaughters:
Chamya, Akina, Ania, and Lavender
You can treasure the practices in this book just as your mothers did.
Grandma loves you! God Bless You!

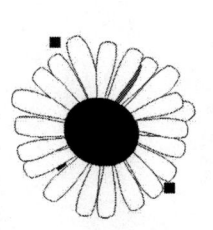

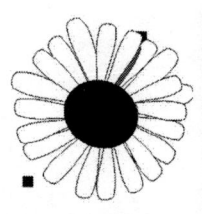

Foreword

The content on the pages of this book comes straight from the heart of a woman who demonstrates an ability to break the communication barriers that can plague mothers and daughters. It is a treasure of information that awakens a mother's instincts for open dialogue with their daughters, and inspires daughters to love and respect their bodies.

Dorothy Webb of Seattle, Washington
(mother of three)

Calling All Girls is an excellent resource for fathers who don't have any female influence to help guide their daughters with things they may go through concerning their girl bodies. Any father that's in this position should have this book. It will educate their daughters in a healthy manner instead of them receiving information from negative outside influences such as peers and media.

John Jamerson of Detroit, Michigan
(father of six)

This book is understanding because it's teaching you about your body and preparing you for life and your menstrual cycle. It may seem scary to some girls, but now they don't have to be afraid. Girls can feel beautiful and practice good hygiene.

Akina Wellere of Oak Park, Michigan
(Student—The Roeper School)

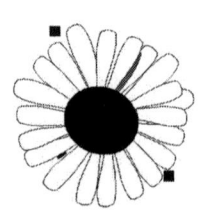

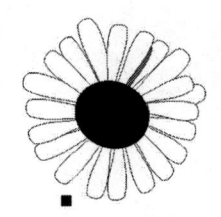

Acknowledgements

To my Heavenly Father: Thank you for preparing me for this awesome journey. Without you, this book would not have come to fruition.

To my husband, Mathew R. Baker: Honey, your love, prayers, and encouragement made all the difference. Thanks for respecting my quiet time and being there when I needed you. May the Peace and Power of God overtake you. I love you.

To my mother, Susie McCarroll: You provided for me as best you could. You were always a praying woman, and I know that I made it off of your prayers. Even when I didn't know the Lord for myself, you prayed for me and remained patient through my trials and errors. I thank you from the bottom of my heart. I love you very much.

To my daughters, Aisha, Tandekile, Anika, and Nyasha: I love you! It is truly an honor to be your mother. It blesses my heart that you all know the LORD. That's the greatest gift a mother can receive. I also appreciate all the sacrifices each of you made to help me pull this book together. To God Be the Glory!

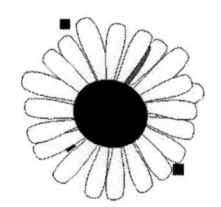

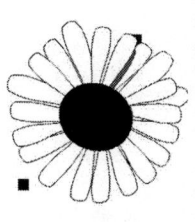

To the Shepherd who nurtured me well, my Spiritual Father, Bishop Jack: I am forever thankful that you took time to view the draft of *Calling All Girls*. I appreciate the many confessions you fed your flock. The confession, "I am an awesome spirit being with infinite potential on the inside," ignited the fire inside of me! The overflowing unconditional love you gave is written in the depths of my heart. I love you dad!

> "I have two daughters and I've read many books.
> There aren't many books out there like this.
> This is good, girls will be blessed by it."
>
> —Bishop Jack C. Wallace—
> Detroit World Outreach, Founding Pastor

To my Spiritual Momma, Pastor Gael Wallace: Thank you for your smile and the great character of a godly woman, an example I choose to follow. I love you!

To my Pastors Benjamin and Charisse Gibert: You are the most dynamic teachers I've ever known. The truth of Gods word and the foundation of your teachings have made all the difference in my Christian walk. The principals you've taught have prepared me for my journey towards fulfilling my God-given destiny. I'm honored to be under your Pastorial care. Thank you so much! I love and appreciate you for being real and all about God's business.

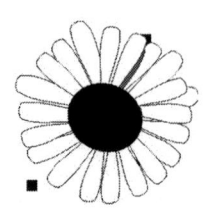

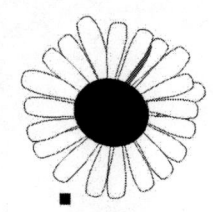

A special thanks to my reading pool, Akina, Thomas, Gloria, Pastor Mike, Dorothy and John.
May God bless you richly for your sacrifice.

To my childhood girlfriend, Karen Dawson: You embraced me at a frightening time in my life when I was 13 years of age and had not a clue of what my menstrual period was. Thank you so much. I thank God for you wholeheartedly. Wherever you are, love, your old friend, Becky McCarroll.

To graphic artists Teresa Hobson and Othoniel Ortiz: thank you for doing such a fine job.

Blessings extended to my entire family, friends, clients and co-workers at SMART Transportation!

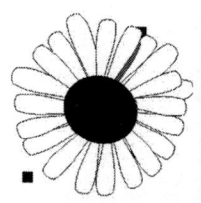

Introduction

Calling All Girls is designed to give females prior knowledge of what to expect as their physical bodies blossom into womanhood. As they learn how to understand who they are as an individual, set standards to live by, and to keep a positive attitude; they will have a high self-esteem, and will make better choices.

The goal of this book is to inspire females to develop a closer relationship with their parents, guardian, or trusted adult. As they are open for discussion on any subject matter, the bonding begins and verbal communications are improved. Ultimately, as young ladies learn to spend time in developing a consistent life-style of prayer, which is simply talking to God; They will appreciate the quality time spent in intimacy with God and will esteem and honor Him!

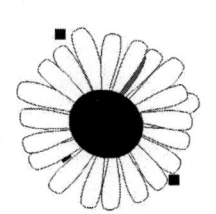

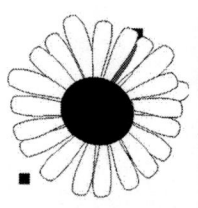

Part 1

Exploring To Know Your Body

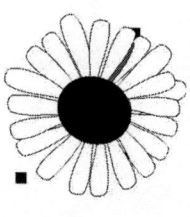

You are unique and one of a kind. There is no one on Earth with your design!

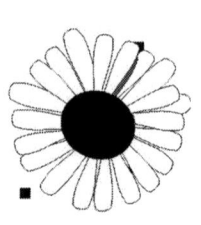

Your Face is Beautiful

Many adolescents have acne breakouts in the form of pimples, blackheads, whiteheads or rashes. This is normal and due to hormone changes. The sebaceous glands that produce excess oil have increased in activity. Regular cleansing is recommended to control the oil; followed by the use of an astringent. As you get older your skin is likely to improve. Although tempting, try to avoid squeezing your pimples because it may cause scarring. If severe breakouts occur, visit a dermatologist (skin doctor) for consultation and treatment. Remember that you are beautiful no matter what the condition of your skin.

Physical Development of Female Maturation

Adolescent girls experience numerous physical body changes. These physical changes are associated with the transition from childhood to womanhood.

Listed below are some physical body developments

- Noticeable growth spurts
- Budding of the breast
- Firmed body physique with curving hips
- Underarm and pubic hair growth

Make it a priority to learn and become familiar with the proper names and functions of your body parts. The main event of puberty is the maturing of the female reproductive system that onsets menstruation.

THE REPRODUCTIVE System: see diagram located in Part 1.

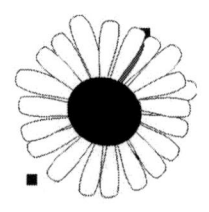

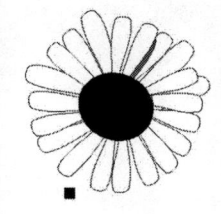

Body designs are unique and are genetically transferred to you!

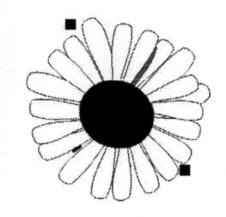

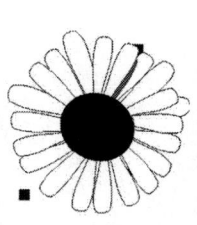

Your Breast

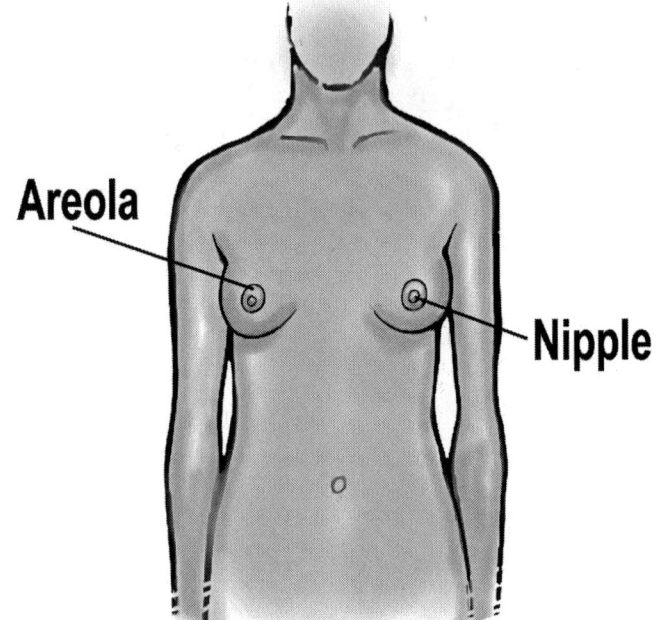

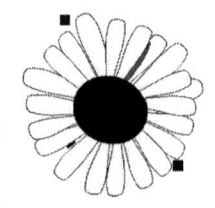

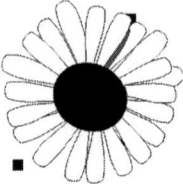

Areola

Nipple

Your breasts are a pair of mammary glands composed of fat cells and tissue developed by hormones. The outer breast composition includes the following:

Nipple—The nipple is a raised area in the center of the breast

Areola—The areola is the pigmented skin surrounding the nipple

Breast size varies from person to person. Some females have breasts that are uneven, one breast larger than the other. This isn't unusual, however discuss concerns with a gynecologist (female specialist).

*A padded bra helps to even out the size.

Developing breasts need the support of a bra to keep from flopping down. If you begin to feel uncomfortable with your breast showing through your shirt or if they are bothersome during sports, its probably time for you to start wearing a bra. You start off with a training bra and as your breast size increase you'll need to be properly fitted for a larger more supportive bra.

Bra sizes have a number and a letter. The number represents the width around your rib cage and the letter represents your cup size. For proper fitting, it's recommended to visit a store that specializes in quality bra sales.
Bra World is an excellent store that can fit your needs as well as your local mainstream department stores. Visit Bra World at www.braworld.ws. Bra World has a great link called Fitting Room, which shows you how to calculate your proper bra size.

Development of your Breast

My first training bra

Age _____ Size _____ Date _____

Who took me to buy it _____

My first real bra

Age _____ Size _____ Date _____

Who took me to buy it _____

Bra size changes

Age _____ New Size _____ Date _____

Age _____ New Size _____ Date _____

Age _____ New Size _____ Date _____

Age _____ New Size _____ Date _____

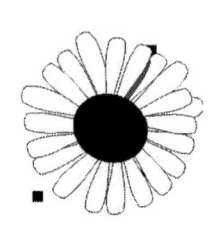

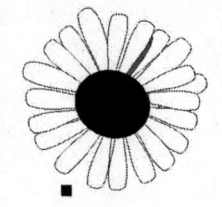

Becoming Familiar With Me

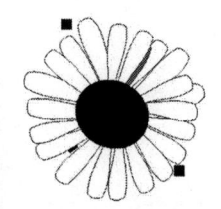

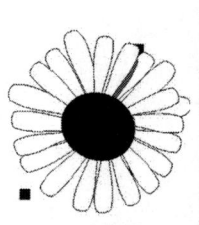

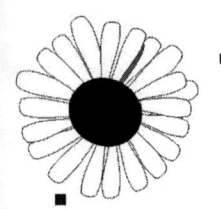

The Female Reproductive System

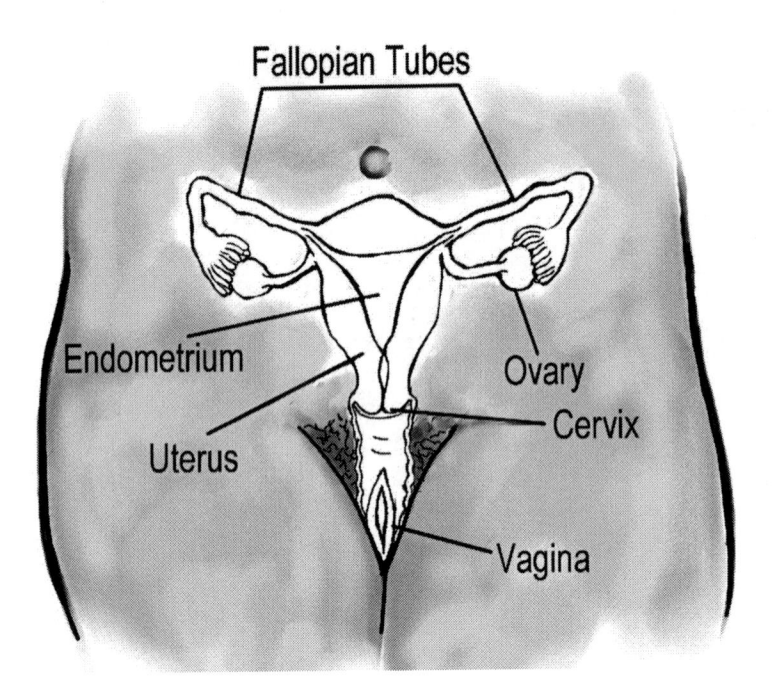

The Internal Reproductive Organs Consist of Ovaries, Fallopian Tubes, Endometrium, Uterus, Cervix and Vagina

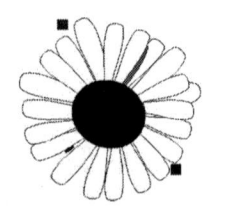

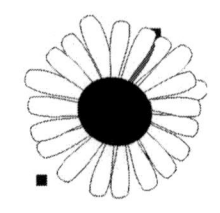

Internal Side View of Anatomy

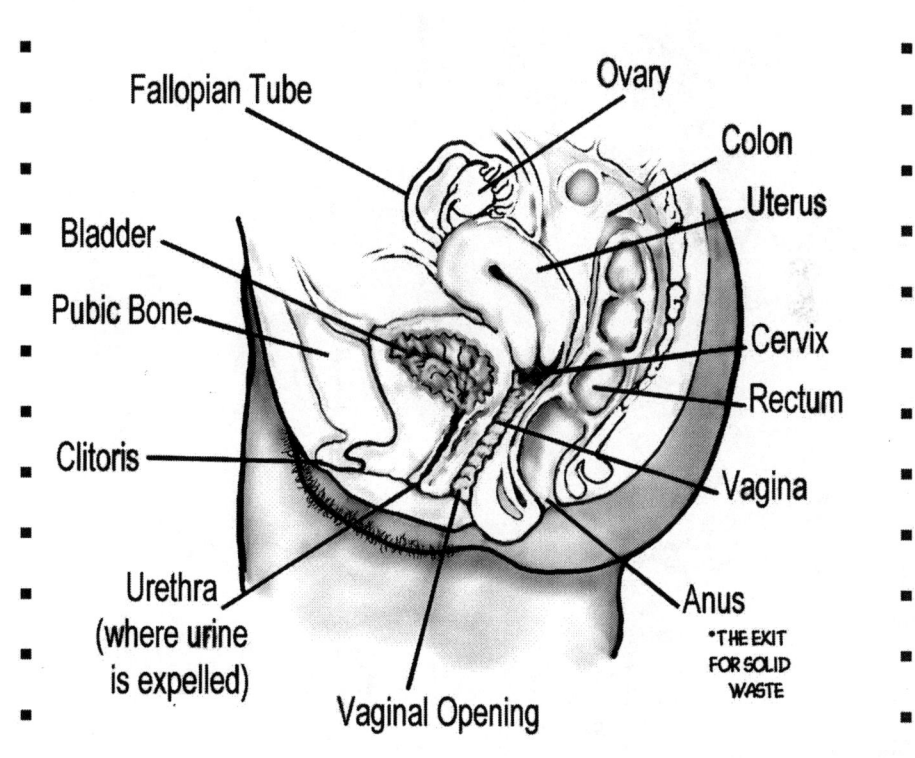

- Fallopian Tube
- Ovary
- Colon
- Uterus
- Bladder
- Pubic Bone
- Cervix
- Rectum
- Clitoris
- Vagina
- Urethra (where urine is expelled)
- Anus *THE EXIT FOR SOLID WASTE
- Vaginal Opening

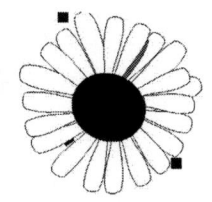

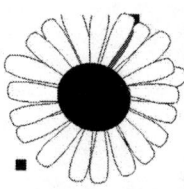

The Private Area of Your Female Body, That's Located Between Your Inner Thighs, Is Called The Vulva

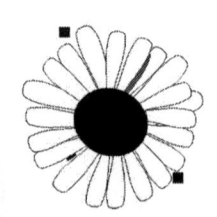

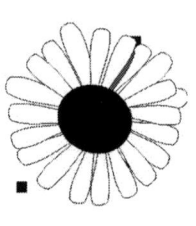

The Vulva

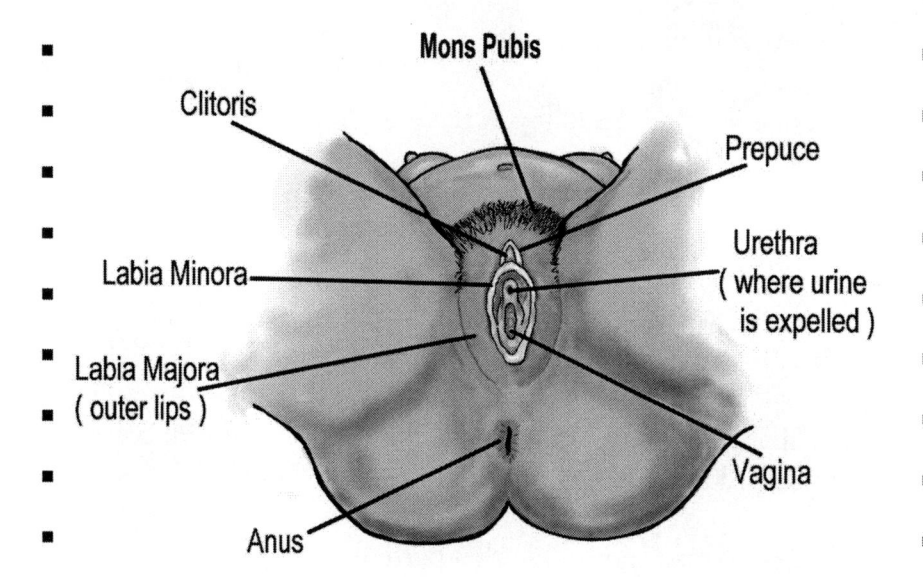

- Clitoris
- Mons Pubis
- Prepuce
- Urethra (where urine is expelled)
- Labia Minora
- Labia Majora (outer lips)
- Vagina
- Anus

External parts of the female reproductive system are located outside of your body.

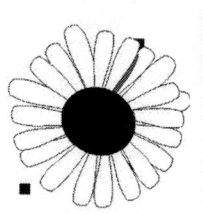

Terms Defined

- Vulva—the external parts of a female's genitals, the lips

- Mons Pubis—the cushioning of fat covering the pubic bone, its covering is with skin and hair

- Labia majora—the outer lips with smooth inner surface, they protect the opening of the vagina

- Labia minora—the inner lips

- Clitoris—a sensitive small organ located on the top of the inner labia, covered with hooded shaped skin

- Vaginal opening—a passage way that leads to the reproductive organs inside your body

- Hymen—a thin layer of skin that partially covers the opening of the vagina in most females

Organs that eliminate fluids and solids are:

- Urethra—a tiny opening where the urine leaves the body

- Anus—The opening to the rectum, and exit for solid waste to leave the body

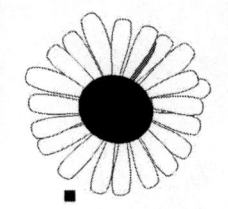

Have you noticed any changes in your body? If so, write down what changed and the age it occurred

Age _____ Noticeable Physical Changes _____

Age _____ Noticeable Physical Changes _____

Age _____ Noticeable Physical Changes _____

Age _____ Noticeable Physical Changes _____

Age _____ Noticeable Physical Changes _____

Age _____ Noticeable Physical Changes _____

Age _____ Noticeable Physical Changes _____

Age _____ Noticeable Physical Changes _____

Age _____ Noticeable Physical Changes _____

Age _____ Noticeable Physical Changes _____

Age _____ Noticeable Physical Changes _____

Age _____ Noticeable Physical Changes _____

Age _____ Noticeable Physical Changes _____

Age _____ Noticeable Physical Changes _____

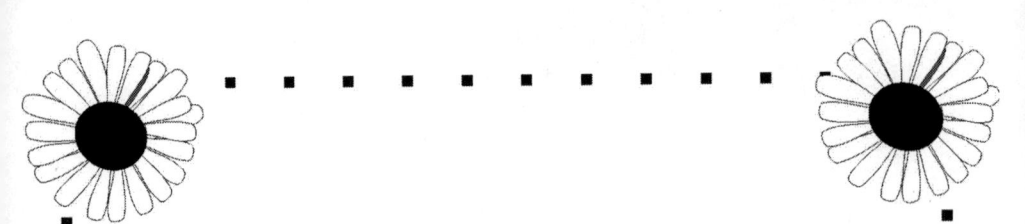

Notes

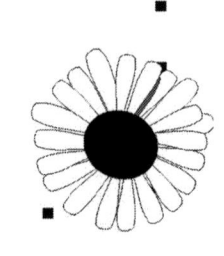

Part 2
Understanding Puberty- Knowledge Is Power

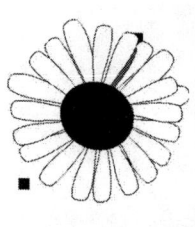

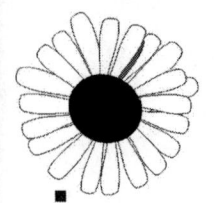

Puberty

Puberty is the period between childhood and adolescence when the hormones estrogen and progesterone are awaken to activity, causing developments of the reproductive system to occur. These female hormones cause growth spurts, breast development, and hair growth in the pubic area and under arms. When a young girl notices her breast budding and hair growing on her body, menstruation is coming soon (approximately within a year). Awaken hormones, estrogen and progesterone may affect you emotionally having ups and downs as your body adjust to development and changes.

Sometimes body odors will begin as a result of puberty. If this has happened to you, be informed that it's due to an awakening of increased glandular activity of the apocrine glands that release odors from underarm pits, breast, genitals, and the anus. This is why consistent personal hygiene is a must.

***If you can smell foul odors on yourself, someone else can smell you too. You don't want it to get to that point so embrace good hygiene. Okay?

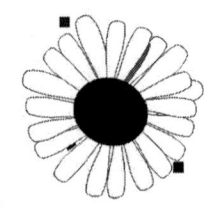

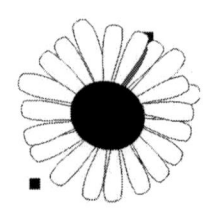

Understanding Terms . . .

Hormones: A chemical substance that are produced by endocrine organs, including the pituitary gland and the gonads (the ovaries in females). They are released into the blood stream and control a whole range of body functions including growth, and reproductive activity.

Estrogen: A hormone produced chiefly in the ovaries that act to regulate certain female reproductive functions and maintains female secondary sex characteristics.

Pituitary Gland: The pituitary gland is a small but very important gland in the base of the brain that secretes hormones.

Endocrine Organs/Glands: The endocrine glands secrete hormones that regulate growth and other important body functions.

Endometrium: The endometrium is the inner glandular layer of the uterus.

Progesterone—a hormone produced in the ovary

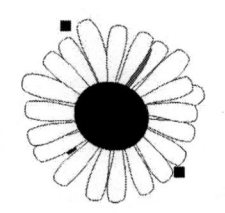

Understanding Menstruation

Menstruation is a normal healthy function of the body. It's triggered by a gland located in the brain called the pituitary gland. The brain produces chemicals that travel in the blood to the ovaries. Once this chemical reach one of the ovaries, the reproductive system begins to function. One of the ovaries releases an egg, it enters the fallopian tube traveling to the uterus that has a lining of blood and tissue called endometrium. Changes during your menstrual cycle take place in the uterine lining. It is this process of menstruation that involves the loss of blood by which the lining of the uterus is shed. Menstruation is the flow of blood and tissue that has a wet feel appearing pinkish, reddish or even brownish in color. Some girls' periods flow light while others may flow heavy.

Q: How old will I be when I start a menstrual cycle?
A: Every girls body is unique. There is no set time for this life-changing event. The onset was different for each of my daughters. Their ages were 8, 9, 14, and 15 years old. As you can see no one was at the same time.

Q: How long will my cycle flow?
A: Again, it varies from person to person. It can flow from 3 days or more. However, some girls are irregular and can skip months. You may also experience a clear mucous flow before or after your cycle has stopped. Don't be alarmed. It's normal. If necessary, use a panty liner.

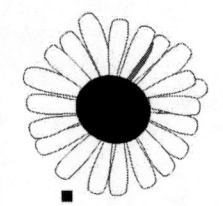

Your Breast may become very tender to touch, causing discomfort, prior to and during your menstrual cycle. If this occurs wear a looser fitting bra for comfort. After your menstrual cycle has ended your breast will return back to normal.

Please understand that you're not ill when your menstrual period begins. You're perfectly normal. If you notice any signs of abnormal spotting or flow in your panties or when wiping with tissue, remain calm and immediately inform your mother or a responsible adult. Adults understand because of experience.

Remember to be of good cheer! It's okay to cry, but not for long, you'll endure this new challenge gracefully!

GIRLS

Your precious bodies are already experiencing or will soon have a menstrual cycle.

A girls' body is capable of childbearing once her menstruation begins.
Keep in mind that childbearing should take place after marriage.

That each one of you should know how to possess (control, manage) his own body in consecration (purity, seperated from things profane) and honor.

I Thessolonians 4:4(AMP)

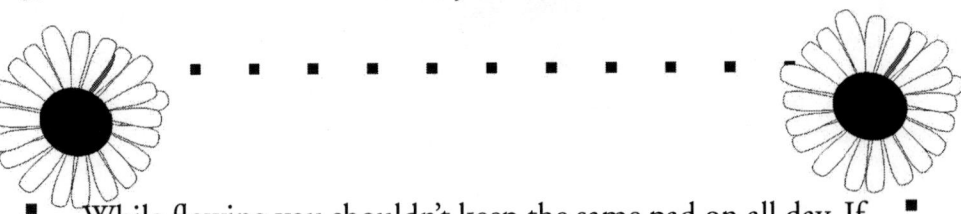

While flowing you shouldn't keep the same pad on all day. If you keep a pad on for too long you'll feel sticky and wet with a smelly odor. Learning how often to change your pad will come with practice. (Note) whether there is light drainage or a normal flow if the panty liner or pad is not timely changed it will kick off an odor.

Do Not flush a pad down the toilet it will clog and stop up the plumbing. Place soiled pad in a sanitary napkin bag, paper towel or plastic, after wrapped, throw it in the garbage.

PRACTICE GOOD HABITS AT ALL TIMES!

Note: Should an overflow accident occur—you don't want it to be on your favorite underwear, so while you are on your period don't wear them.

Common Names Your Menstrual Cycle is Known By . . .

Period

Monthly　　　Cycle

Time of The Month

On The Rag　　　　　　　　　　　Aunt Flow

Code Red　　　　　　　Red Alert

Cycling

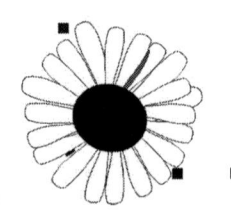

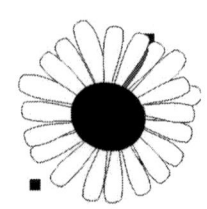

Diagram of
The Reproductive System
As it Relates to Menstruation

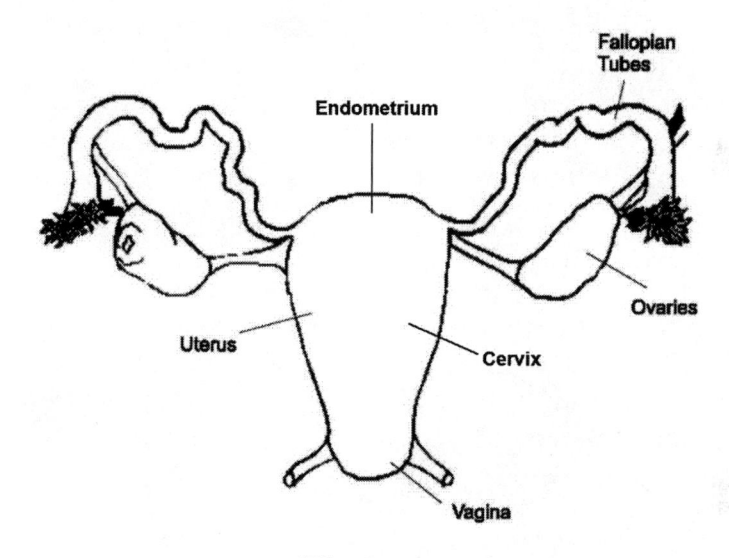

Fallopian Tubes

Endometrium

Uterus

Ovaries

Cervix

Vagina

The Process

Ovaries—release an egg

Fallopian Tubes—where the egg travels to the uterus

Uterus—where the lining of blood and tissue called endometrium is located. This is where changes take place in the uterine lining, which is the process of menstruation

Vagina—the exit for the flow of the uterine lining, blood and tissue

Cervix—the neck of the uterus that extends into the top of the vagina

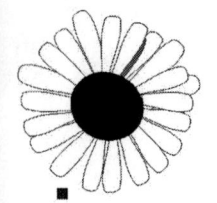

All About PMS
(Pre menstrual Syndrome)

PMS is a hormonal change that takes place in your body right before your cycle begins. It can cause both physical and psychological symptoms. These altering reactions are due to hormonal fluctuations that take place in your body. During this time, it is not uncommon to have a few pimples, nosebleeds, tender breast, cramping, headaches, or backaches.

If by chance you experience PMS you will learn how to adjust by finding a time and place for rest. Always discuss your concerns and how you're feeling with your mother, guardian, or a delegated adult. They will assist you in ways to relieve any discomfort. Be sure to eat less salt during your cycle because it can contribute to swelling of your body.

Physical Changes associated with PMS

Fluid retention—bloating—weight gain—swelling of the hands, feet, legs, abdomen—headaches—swimming in head—backache—abdominal cramps—constipation—gastritis—loss of appetite—food cravings—increased appetite—chocolate—sweets—etc.

Psychological Changes associated with PMS

Mood swings—irritable—snappy—touchy—sensitive—crying spells—lack of concentration—tiredness—depression—sleepiness—etc.

Helpful Hints and Practices

1) Keep a daily journal, be consistent. You may have to reflect back if you have unusual cycle patterns or discomfort.

2) You'll need 2 calendars one for your bedroom wall and a pocket calendar for your purse/bookbag.

Why a Calendar?

Planning around your menstrual cycle is a good thing. Listen girls, the calendar will keep you on top of things; meaning It's better to know when it is about to come, rather than to have a surprise visit.
As mentioned earlier, menstrual cycles vary from person to person. Cycles can range from every 26 to 28 days or less.

SO LET'S PLAN AHEAD!!!

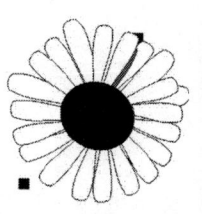

The Calendar Method

26 Day Cycle
1) Mark a circle around the date on your calendar of the very first day your cycle starts, whether it's light spotting or flowing.
2) Count 26 days from the start date and circle it.
3) Write the word start next to the 26th day circle.

28 Day Cycle
1) Mark a circle around the date on your calendar of the very first day your cycle starts, whether it's light spotting or flowing.
2) Count 28 days from the start date and circle it.
3) Write the word start next to the 28th day circle.

Your menstrual cycle will usually start on the 26th or 28th day that is marked. After you've had a menstrual cycle for 2 consecutive months, you should be able to determine whether your cycle is 26, 28 days or less. Every girl's body is different.

Some girls may be irregular by skipping months. This isn't unusual, however, if concerned, seek medical attention.

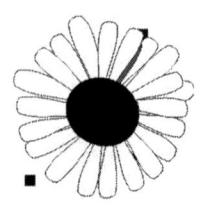

The Calendar Method
(See Example of Calendar)
Example of a 26 day and 28 day cycle

Menstruation start day is on the 3rd of September. Write start and place a circle around the 3rd this will be the 1st day of your cycle. Then count from that date to 26 and 28th day which will be September 28 and 30th, this is when your next period should start . . .

Notice in September there are 2 menstrual cycles, that's because you started flowing early in the month. This will not occur every month. It depends on how the date fall.

Now wasn't that easy?

Practice make perfect. Lets pretend your cycle is a 28 day cycle. Count from September 30th into the next month October for 28 days, October the 26th would be your next start date

Try planning 3 months ahead, although you can pre-count for as many months as you please.

Another good practice is to mark an end date of your cycle on your calendar.

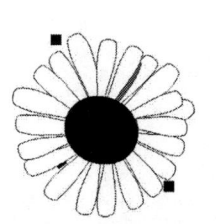

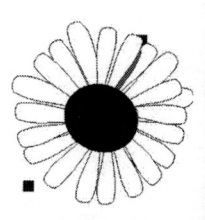

EXAMPLE OF CALENDER METHOD

SEPTEMBER

SUN	MON	TUE	WED	THUR	FRI	SAT
				1	2	(3) Start Day 1
4	5	6	7	8	9	10
11	12	13	14	15	16	17
18	19	20	21	22	23	24
25	26	27	(28) Start 26 Days	29	(30) Start 28 Days	31

OCTOBER

SUN	MON	TUE	WED	THUR	FRI	SAT
						1
2	3	4	5	6	7	8
9	10	11	12	13	14	15
16	17	18	19	20	21	22
23	24	25	(26) Start 28 Days	27	28	29
30						

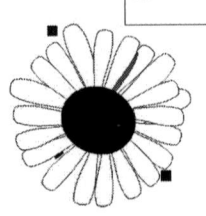

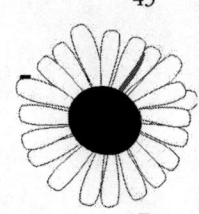

Girl Essentials

Preparation:
1. A package of sanitary napkins (pads)
2. Moist disposable wipes
3. A small shoulder purse
4. Baby Powder
5. Panty liners
6. (Optional) disposable panties
7. Pocket calendar

Try different types of pads, you'll find the one most comfortable. They have a self-stick adhesive to secure them in your undergarments.

(Pad types in size)
Panty liners—light flow
regular pads—light flow to normal flow
super pads—heavy flow

*Note: Remember to take extra pads and moist wipes with you while away from home.

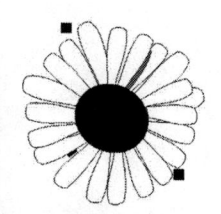

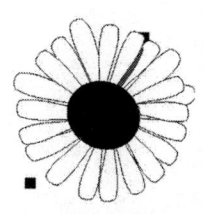

12 Month Flow Chart

Menstrual Record Chart

| S | Spotting | L | Light | N | Normal | ■ | Heavy | E | End |

Mark in the boxes below to describe your flow in the year of _____

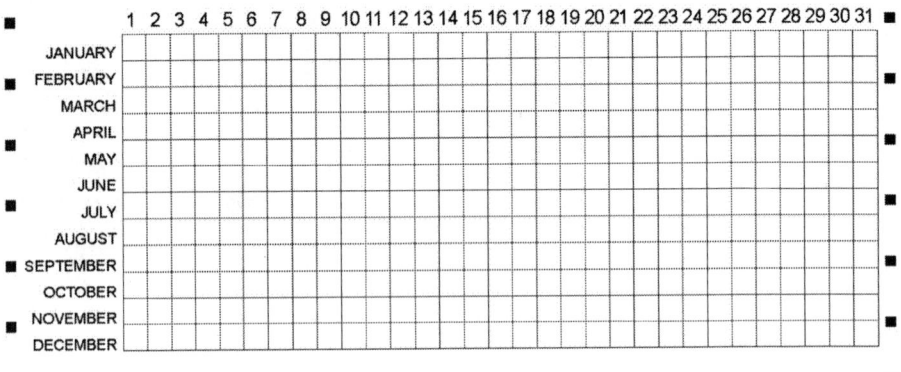

	1 2 3 4 5 6 7 8 9 10 11 12 13 14 15 16 17 18 19 20 21 22 23 24 25 26 27 28 29 30 31
JANUARY	
FEBRUARY	
MARCH	
APRIL	
MAY	
JUNE	
JULY	
AUGUST	
SEPTEMBER	
OCTOBER	
NOVEMBER	
DECEMBER	

Example

	1 2 3 4 5 6 7 8 9 10 11 12 13 14 15 16 17 18 19 20 21 22 23 24 25 26 27 28 29 30 31
DECEMBER	S L L ■ N E

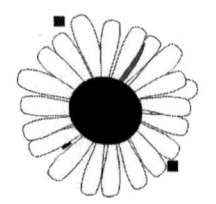

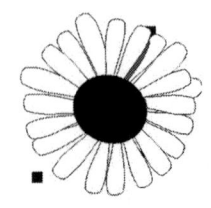

My Keepsake Record

I was _____ years old when my menstruation cycle began.

The date was _____ at _____ o'clock.

On that day I was doing _____
_____

I was wearing _____

My first reaction was _____
_____

The first person I told was _____

Was I prepared? Yes ___ No ___

I will keep track of my cycle by journaling!

Signature _____
Date _____

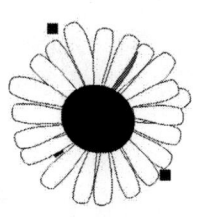

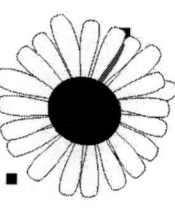

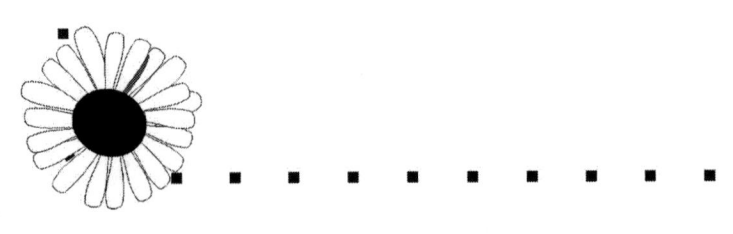

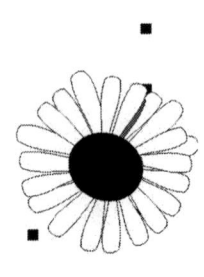

Notes

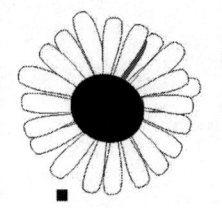

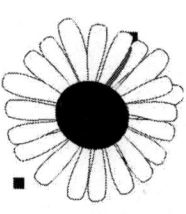

Part 3
Teen Info

Visiting the Gynecologist

Now that your body has changed and matured, it's time to schedule an appointment for an examination with a female specialist (Gynecologist).

According to American College of Obstetricians and Gynecologist. It is recommended that you should have your first ob-gyn visit between age 13 and 15. Talk to your mom, aunt, sister, or guardian as to what to expect at your visit. It's normal to feel a little nervous about your first visit, but knowing what to expect will make you feel a little more at ease.

Your doctor will ask many questions. This will allow you to be cared for in the best possible way. Be sure to answer all questions honestly because its for your benefit.

On your first visit, you and your doctor may only talk. It allows the patient and doctor to get to know each other. Establishing a relationship with your doctor is a way to build trust and it makes it easier for you to ask questions. Don't worry, doctors have a duty to keep patient information confidential so feel free to discuss anything. Sometimes it is easy to forget what you were going to ask the doctor, so try to write down your questions in advance.

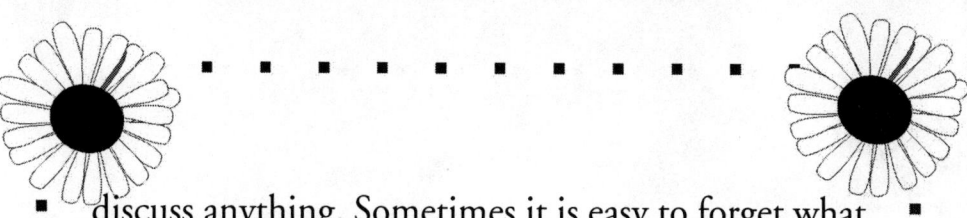

It is also possible for you to have certain exams on your first visit, depending on your age, or if you're experiencing any problems. Common tests include: general physicals, pelvic exams, breast exams, and pap tests. Your doctor will explain in more detail what the test is and how it is performed. If your parents ask your doctor questions concerning your exam, the doctor will remind them of your privacy.

Young ladies, yearly visits to the Gynecologist are essential in maintaining a healthy female body. Talk to your parents/guardian and remember to take good care of your body!

TERMS DEFINED

OB-stands for Obstetric: It means to stand before; pertaining to the delivery of women in childbed.
OBSTETRICIAN-one skilled in the art of assisting women in parturition (being delivered of young).
GYN-stands for Gynecology: It is the medical science of the functions and diseases peculiar to women.
GYNECOLOGIST-Female specialist

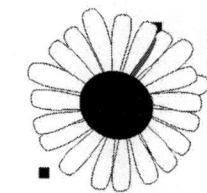

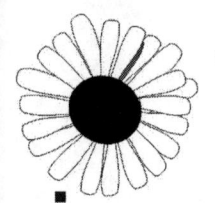

Example of a Pelvic Exam

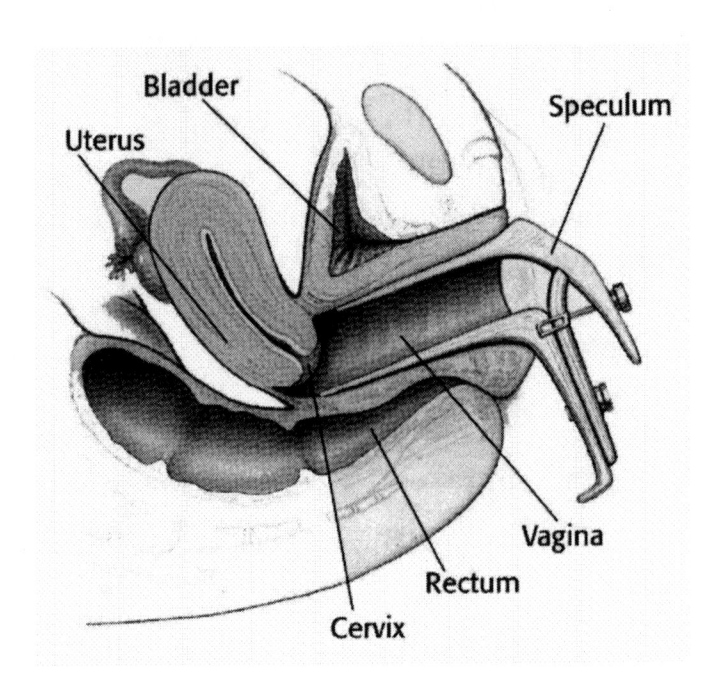

Figure: Cross-section diagram labeled with Bladder, Uterus, Speculum, Vagina, Rectum, and Cervix.

For the pelvic exam, a device called a speculum may be used to help look at the cervix and vagina. It is placed into the vagina to hold open the vaginal walls. You will feel some pressure when the speculum opens.

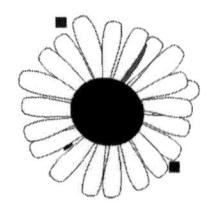

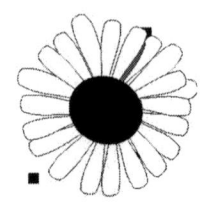

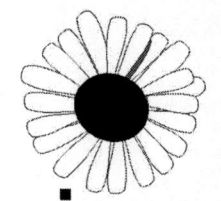

Example of a Pelvic Exam

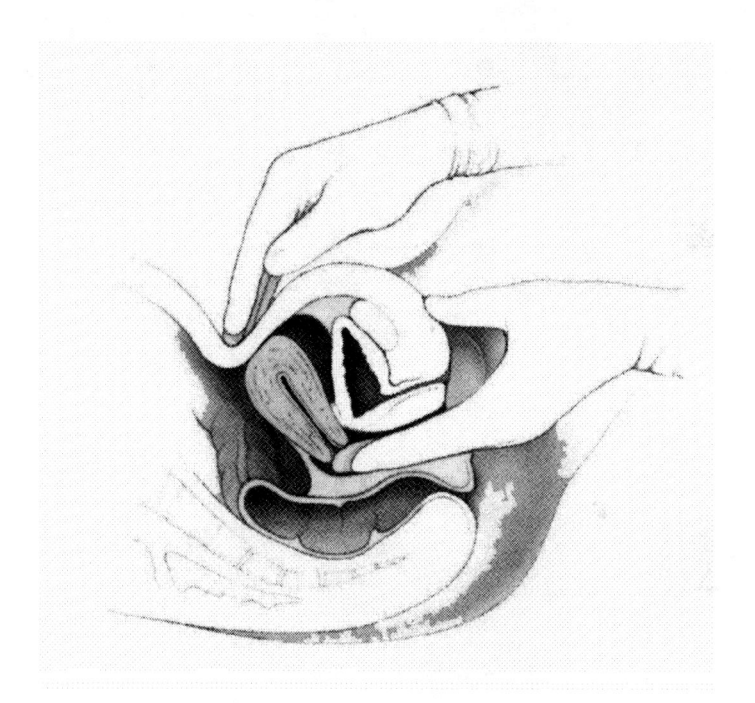

The doctor may also do an exam of the internal organs, Including the rectum and vagina. The doctor places one or two gloved, lubricated fingers into the vagina and reaches up to the cervix. The other hand presses on the abdomen from the outside. This helps the doctor to check the size, position, and shape of these organs.

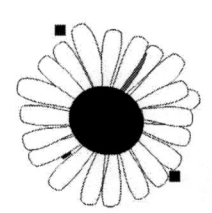

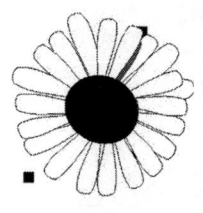

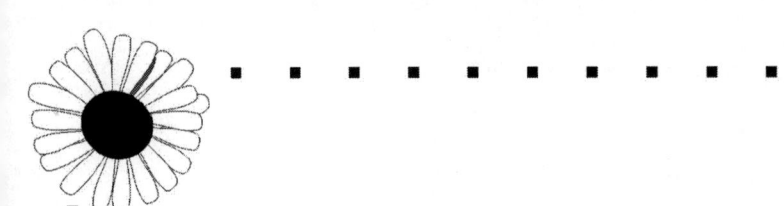

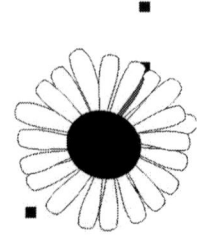

Notes

Part 4

Exploring Personal Hygiene

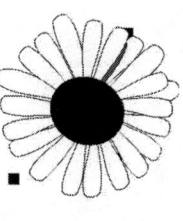

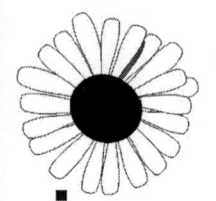

Cleansing Your . . .

FACE
Wipe over your entire face with a warm wash cloth including your eye creases. Proceed washing in a circular motion with soap or cleanser recommended by your parent. Be sure to clean inside and behind the ears also your neck.

TEETH
Brush your teeth daily and after meals to avoid plaque buildup. Promote healthy gums by brushing them also. Gently brush over your tongue and the roof of your mouth, and floss daily to remove food particles from between your teeth. The use of an antiseptic mouthwash helps to eliminate germs. Having a bright winning smile depends on good healthy teeth.

UNDERARMS/BREAST
Wash underarm pit, pat dry then apply deodorant.
Gently wash over your entire breast. Lift each breast cleansing underneath, then pat dry with a towel. Sweating underneath the breast is not uncommon. Odor and possible skin irritation may occur if not cleansed and kept dry.

VULVA The lips of the external female genitalia

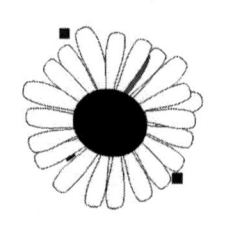

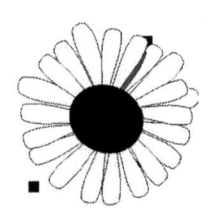

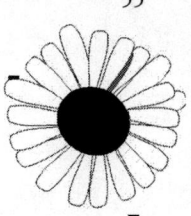

While cleansing your private area (labia) make sure you wash between the creases. Gently pull back the hooded like skin that cover the clitoris to cleanse the accumulations of secretion buildup. Cleanse vagina and pat dry. Perspiration occurs in the genital area because it's closed in a dark area where air doesn't flow. Proper and frequent cleansing is a must to prevent irritation, infection and body odor.

ANUS—Proper wiping

After urinating or having a bowel movement it's important for you to wipe from the front to back. The reason for this is because stool (bowel) is bacteria from the digestive tract. Improper wiping can cause irritation and infection in the vaginal area. Make it a practice to wash your bottom (anus) after having a bowel movement. While away from home consider the use of moist disposable wipes.

HYGIENE TIP: when washing your body, utilize two separate wash cloths: one for your face and the other for your body and private areas.

* Note—Shower or bathe daily.
Also remember that you are supposed to wash up the next morning also!
Taking a bath or shower before bedtime does not cover your cleansing for the next day.

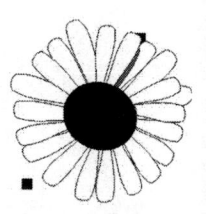

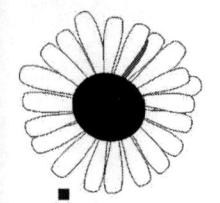

Caring for your . . .

FEET
Keep them clean and dry allowing feet to air out whenever possible.

Care for dryness
Daily soaking helps to eliminate dry skin buildup. After soaking your feet, use a foot file to smooth the skin followed by a moisturizing cream to retain softness.

Cost Saver Tip:
Instead of paying for a professional pedicure (which could be costly), have a foot fellowship with a friend or family member. This is an excellent opportunity to socialize while giving each other a home pedicure.

HANDS
You should thoroughly cleanse your hands constantly throughout the day.
Hands carry lots and lots of germs. Hand washing, when done correctly, is the single most effective way to prevent the spread of communicable diseases.

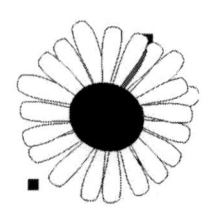

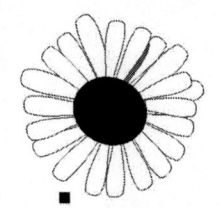

Think about it . . .

You may touch a doorknob that was just touched by a person who coughed or used the bathroom without washing their hands. What if there were traces of fecal matter on their hands. Now you have it on yours. YUCK! You could catch a cold from something like that. This is just one example of how quickly you can pick up germs on your hands. There are many many many more. Whether you urinate or have a bowel movement, it is imperative that you wash your hands after using the bathroom. It's also good to wash your hands before handling food, and touching your face or anyone else's

Useful tips

The following are good practices to develop when using a public restroom:

- Never sit on the toilet without using a toilet liner. If there are none available, pad the seat of the toilet with lots of tissue. Many germs live on toilet seats and you surely don't want to sit on them.
- When it's time to flush, don't touch the handle with your bare hands. Grab some tissue and flush with that, or use your foot. Again, creepy little germs live on the handle. You can also grab tissue to lock and unlock the stall door.
- Make sure you wash your hands after using the restroom. When washing your hands, the "don't touch" policy is a good idea. Grab some paper towel or tissue to dispense soap and to turn the water faucet on and off. Nowadays, many restrooms are equipped with sensored sinks, soap

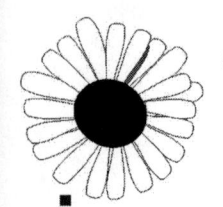

dispensers and paper towel machines. These conveniences are a great way to control the transmittal of germs. Be sure to use the proper handwashing technique listed on the following page.

Proper hand washing technique
There is more to hand washing than you think! By rubbing your hands vigorously with soapy water, you pull the dirt and the oily soils free from your skin. The soap lather suspends both the dirt and germs trapped inside and are then quickly washed away.

Five easy steps to follow:
- Wet your hands with warm running water
- Add soap, and then rub your hands together, making a soapy lather. Do this away from the running water for at least 30 seconds, being careful not to wash the lather away. Wash the front and back of your hands, as well as between your fingers and under your nails.
- Rinse your hands well under warm running water
- Wipe and dry hands well with a single use paper towel
- Turn off water using paper towel.

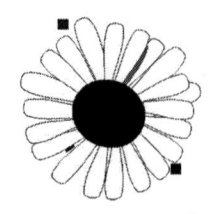

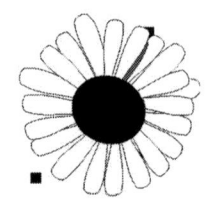

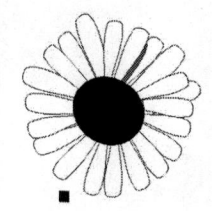

Grooming

Hair Styling

Young ladies do not leave home without styling your hair. If you know you won't have time in the morning, consider styling your hair before bedtime and wear a bonnet or scarf to preserve the style. Keeping your hair clean and combed reflects your outer appearance. It shows that you care about the way you look. You'll feel better, too!

Removal of Underarm and Pubic Hair
(adult supervision is recommended)

Shaving or using hair removal lotions can temporarily remove underarm and pubic hair. These methods remove the surface hair only. Other methods are:

Waxing—removes hair from below the skin surface lasting longer than lotions and shaving.

Laser/Electrolysis—is a permanent hair removal procedure.

NEVER take it upon yourself to try any of the above without adult supervision

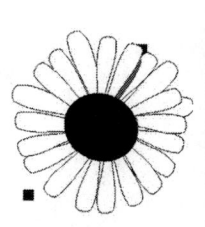

Pamper yourself.

Relax in a warm bubble bath!

To avoid irritation use unscented products:

Bath Oils
Bath Beads
Bubble Bath
Shower Gel
Soaps
Powder
Deodorant
Lotions

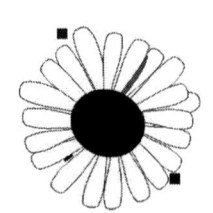

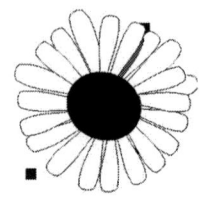

Your Personal Hygiene and Appearance Is A Reflection of You . . .

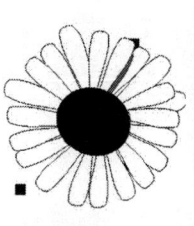

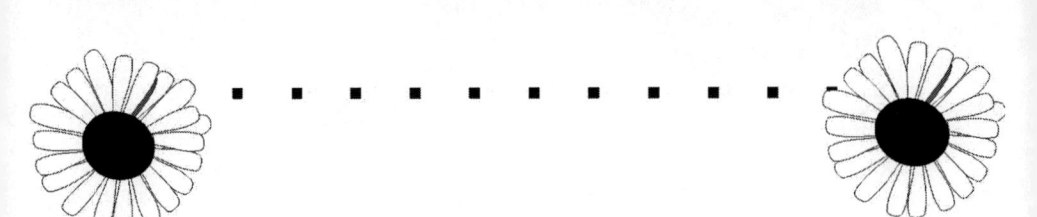

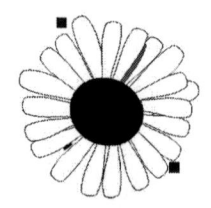

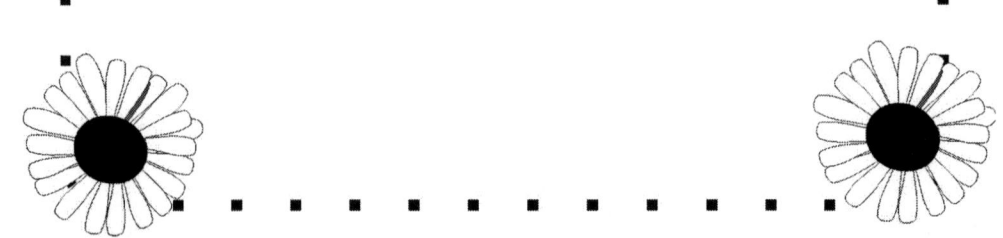

Notes

Part 5

Girl Talk

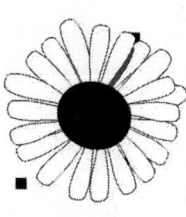

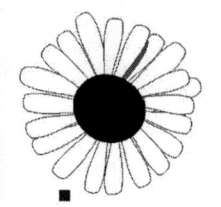

Distractions

HAVING PRIOR KNOWLEDGE WILL PREPARE AND STRENGTHEN YOU

By design, females are compassionate and sensitive. Persuasive words can have a great effect on your emotions. Words spoken are very powerful, and boys are aware of this character trait in girls so they use words to their advantage.

Girls the following are things boys may say to get you to like them or capture your heart:
"You belong to me"—"I love you"—"God made us for each other"—"I need you"—"I want you so bad"—"You're cute"—"You're the most beautiful girl in the world"—"I can't live without you"—"I want you to be my wife"—"We can make a pretty baby together"—"Hey beautiful"—"I'll die if I can't be with you"—"Pretty Lady"—"Foxy Lady"—"let me put a diamond on your finger"—"you mean the world to me"—"We'll be together forever."

CAUTION: It's just sweet talk.

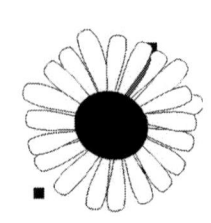

- Love grows over long periods of time well into adulthood
- Having a boy as a friend is okay, physical attractions are normal
- You will meet many boys before adulthood, be obedient and patient
- It's all about how you handle yourself
- Don't be turned on or moved by smooth talk
- Don't let the comments and compliments go to your head

Stay focused! Don't allow distractions to interfere with your beliefs, goals, dreams and aspirations. God has a great plan for your life!

For I know the thoughts and plans that I have for you, says the Lord, thoughts and plans for welfare and peace and not for evil, to give you hope in your final outcome.
Jeremiah 29:11(AMP)

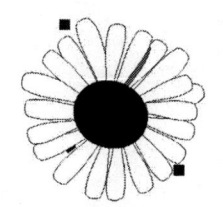

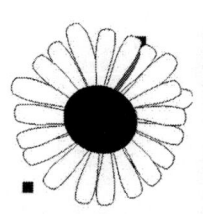

Again, girls listen up! By design, males operate in a task and conquer manner. What this means is that they will do anything or tell you everything they think you may want to hear in order to capture your heart. Although it may seem flattering when a boy goes out of his way to show you that he likes you, in most cases he'll have a hidden agenda. Don't allow yourself to be used or violated by anyone. This includes touching or fumbling on your body parts. If you find yourself in a compromising position, tell that person to back off. Sometimes boys can be very aggressive and your efforts to say no may not go so smoothly. In such cases, get out of that persons presence immediately. Inform your parent or a trusted adult if someone has done you wrong. Never keep it to yourself.

For God did not give us a spirit of timidity (of cowardice, of craven and cringing and fawning fear), but [He has given us a spirit] of power and of love and of calm and well-balanced mind and discipline and self-control.
2 Timothy 1: 7(AMP)

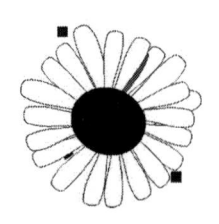

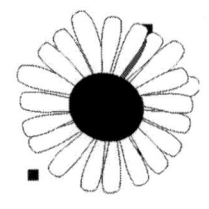

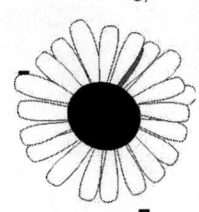

Kissing

There will be times when you may be asked for a kiss. If you allow this to happen, you run the risk of the kiss leading to other things such as hugging, fondling, or intimate acts.

Have Patience and Be Obedient

*SAVE THAT KISS FOR YOUR WEDDING DAY!

♡ ♡ ♡ ♡ ♡ ♡ ♡

NO! NO! NO! Not until marriage!

Hebrews 13:4a (KJV) Marriage is honorable in all,

Hebrews 13:4a (AMP) Let marriage be held in honor (esteemed worthy, precious, of great price, and especially dear) in all things. And thus let the marriage bed be undefiled (kept undishonored);

Marriage: wedlock, the institution by which men and women are joined together and form a family.

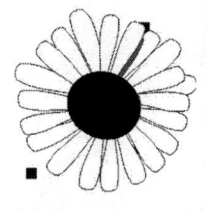

Positive Things To Think About.

When you develop a daily routine, you won't have much time for distractions. Spend as much time as you possibly can thinking about positive things that will make your life better. Consider creating a list of positive things you'd like to focus on. The following is a starter list for you to begin thinking about:

Create your list of positive things . . .

1. Practice a consistent prayer life
2. Exercise daily
3. Maintain healthy eating habits
4. Focus on new things and ideas
5. Set goals for myself
6. Be honest at all times
7. Utilize my time wisely
8. Spend time with my family
9. Study consistently and keep up with my homework
10. Stay focused in school
11. Graduate from High School and continue my education
12. Be selective with my friends
13. Encourage others
14. Invest and save my money
15. Don't give in to peer pressure

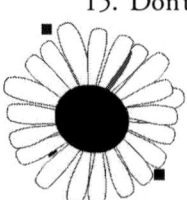

Words to the Wise

Be selective with your friends. Don't hang out with negative people. If you do, eventually you'll display some of the same behaviors. Positive friendships are great for your personal growth.

Ladies, you've reached a milestone from childhood to young adulthood. Around the age of 18 years you may begin to think.

Where Do I Go From Here?

"Where do I go from here?" The best place to start is establishing a good prayer life. In these years to come you'll need lots of encouragement to make it through. Praying is simply talking to God. As you learn to spend time just talking to God, you'll develop an intimate relationship with Him. It is this relationship that will give you the peace and wisdom needed to make it through the many challenges that will come.

I have strength for all things in Christ Who empowers me [I am ready for anything and equal to anything through Him Who infuses inner strength into me; I am self-sufficient in Christ's sufficiency].
Philippians 4:13(AMP)

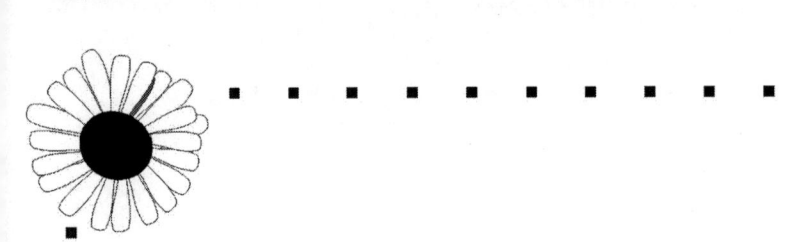

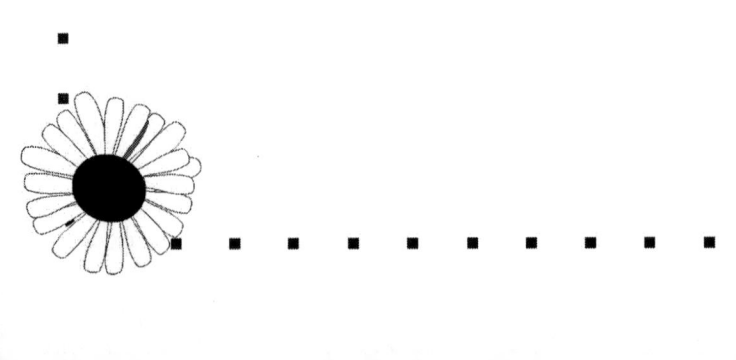

Notes

Part 6

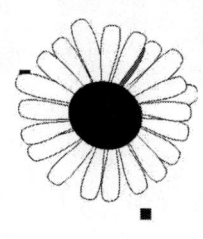

Begin Your Day with a daily Prayer . . . God loves to hear "your" voice when "you" PRAY!

7 Days Of Prayer

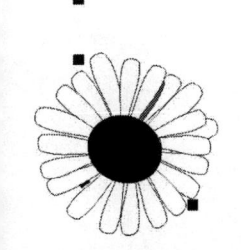

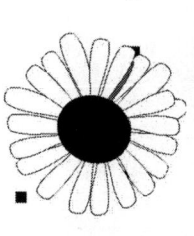

Sunday

LORD, give me a mind to pray. With so many things I face everyday I need balance so that I won't forget about you. LORD teach me while I'm young how to seek You and pray more.

AMEN

Take out some time to make up your own prayer to God . . .

My Sunday Prayer:

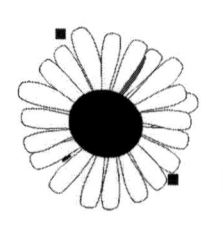

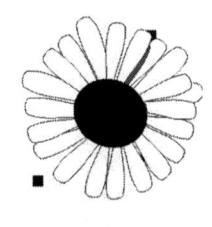

_____
_____
_____
_____
_____
_____
_____
_____

Show me Your ways, O Lord; teach me Your paths.
Psalms 25:4 (AMP)

Monday

LORD, I thank You for my own style and look. I know You look at the inward part of me and don't judge me by the outer appearance. LORD teach me how to look like a representative of You.

AMEN

My Monday Prayer:

_____
_____
_____
_____
_____
_____
_____
_____

I [the Lord] will instruct you and teach you in the way you should go; I will counsel you with My eye upon you.

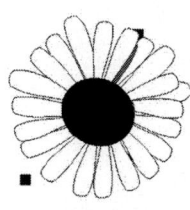

Psalms 32:8 (AMP)

Tuesday

LORD, today help me to have more personal conversations with You than I do on the telephone. Help me to fill any communication gap that we may have, LORD I want more of You.

AMEN

My Tuesday Prayer:

_____
_____
_____
_____
_____
_____
_____
_____
_____

In the morning You hear my voice, O Lord; in the morning I prepare [a prayer, a sacrifice] for You and watch and wait [for You to speak to my heart].

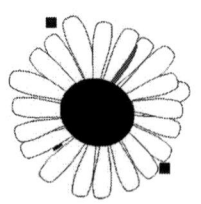

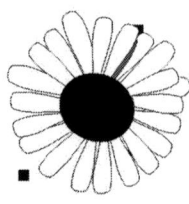

Psalms 5:3 (AMP)

Wednesday

LORD, today I woke up thinking about my life. Teach me how to keep my mind stayed on You, instead of the issues I face each day. LORD give me a life of peace and understanding.

AMEN

My Wednesday Prayer:

_____
_____
_____
_____
_____
_____
_____
_____
_____

Lead me, O Lord, in Your righteousness because of my enemies; make Your way level (straight and right) before my face.

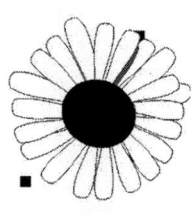

Psalms 5:8 (AMP)

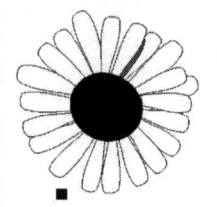

Thursday

LORD, sometimes I don't feel my best, but You always bring me through no matter how I feel. I'm glad You love me in spite of my everyday feelings and thoughts, LORD I thank You so much.

AMEN

My Thursday Prayer:

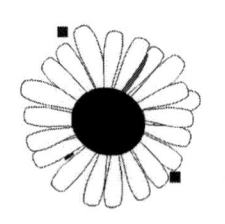

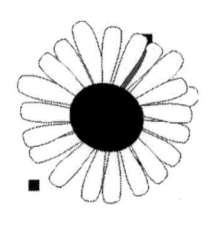

_____
_____
_____
_____
_____
_____
_____
_____
_____

Hear my voice O God, in my prayer: preserve my life from fear of the enemy.

Psalms 64:1 (KJV)

Friday

LORD, I'm happy to be a part of this day because You made it. I'm so glad to have You in my life. Because of Your love, I'm learning to love myself as a daughter of the King.

AMEN

My Friday Prayer:

_____
_____
_____
_____
_____
_____
_____
_____
_____

Oh Lord, our Lord, how excellent (majestic and glorious) is Your name in all the earth!

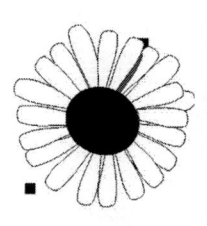

Psalms 8:9 (AMP)

Saturday

Today LORD every time I think of you I will smile because I am somebody to you; and no matter what my day is like, You'll bring me through. I'm learning that a simple smile can brighten not only my day but someone else's too. LORD I thank You for happiness and the gift of love.

AMEN

My Saturday Prayer:

_____
_____
_____
_____
_____
_____
_____
_____

It is a good thing to give thanks unto the Lord, and to sing praises unto thy name, O most High: To show forth thy lovingkindness in the morning, and thy faithfulness every night,

Psalms 92:1-2 (KJV)

Give Thanks To God For All Things and Pray (Morning—Noon—Night)

The Golden Rule

Keep on asking and it will be given to you; Keep on seeking and you will find; keep on knocking [reverently] and [the door] will be opened to you. For everyone who keeps on asking receives; and he who keeps on seeking finds; and to him who keeps on knocking, [the door] will be opened.

Matthew 7:7-8(AMP)

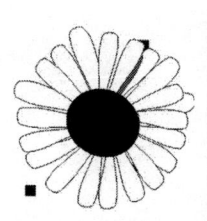

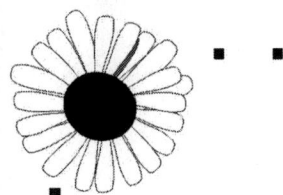

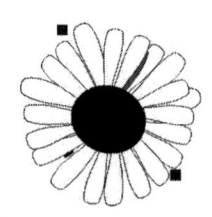

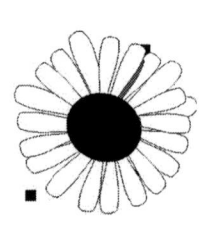

Notes

Part 7

Scriptures AND Encouragement To guide you

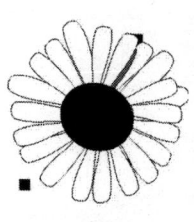

Blessings for Obedience

Deuteronomy 28: 1-14(AMP)

1. If you will listen diligently to the voice of the Lord your God, being watchful to do all His commandments which I command you this day, the Lord your God will set you high above all the nations of the earth.
2. And all these blessings shall come upon you and overtake you if you heed the voice of the Lord your God.
3. Blessed shall you be in the city and blessed shall you be in the field.
4. Blessed shall be the fruit of your body and the fruit of your ground and the fruit of your beasts, the increase of your cattle and the young of your flock.
5. Blessed shall be your basket and your kneading trough.
6. Blessed shall you be when you come in and blessed shall you be when you go out.

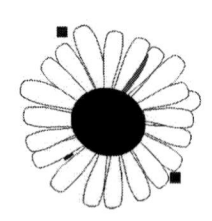

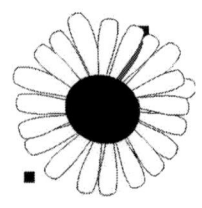

7 The Lord shall cause your enemies who rise up against you to be defeated before your face; they shall come out against you one way and flee before you seven ways.

8 The Lord shall command the blessing upon you in your storehouse and in all that you undertake. And He will bless you in the land which the Lord your God gives you.

9 The Lord will establish you as a people holy to Himself, as He has sworn to you, if you keep the commandments of the Lord your God, and walk in His ways.

10 And all people of the earth shall see that you are called by the name [and in the presence of] the Lord, and they shall be afraid of you.

11 And the Lord shall make you have a surplus of prosperity, through the fruit of your body, of your live-stock, and of your ground, in the land which the Lord swore to your fathers to give you.

12 The Lord shall open to you His good treasury, the heavens, to give the rain of your land in its season

and to bless all the work of your hands; and you shall lend to many nations, but you shall not borrow.

13 And the Lord shall make you the head, and not the tail; and you shall be above only, and you shall not be beneath, if you heed the commandments of the Lord your God which I command you this day and are watchful to do them.

14 And you shall not turn aside from any of the words which I command you this day, to the right hand or to the left, to go after other gods to serve them.

Honor Your Parents

Children, obey your parents in the Lord: for this is right. Honour thy Father and Mother; which is the first commandment with promise; That it may be well with thee, and thou mayest live long on the earth.

Ephesians 6:1-3(KJV)

Honoring Parents involves more than obedience . . .
It involves Respect and Appreciation
                So Show It!

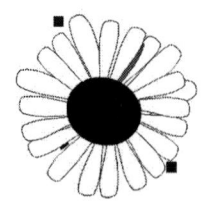

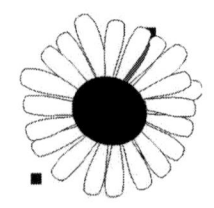

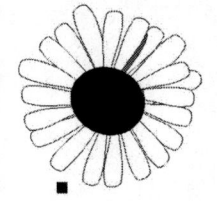

Laws followed gives peace and good reward . . .

The Ten Commandments

Found In *Exodus 20:1-17* **and** *Deut 28:1-14*

1. Thou shalt have no other gods before me.
2. Thou shalt not make unto thee any graven image.
3. Thou shalt not take the name of the Lord thy God in vain.
4. Remember the sabbath day, to keep it holy.
5. Honour thy father and thy mother.
6. Thou shalt not kill.
7. Thou shalt not commit adultery.
8. Thou shalt not steal.
9. Thou shalt not bear false witness against thy neighbor.
10. Thou shalt not covet.

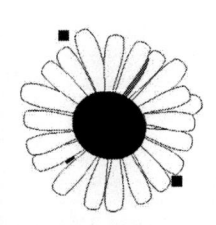

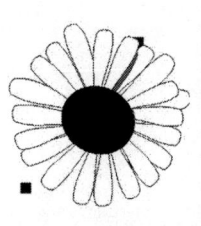

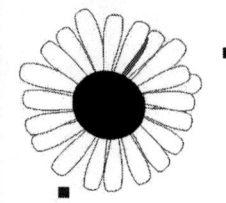

True Happiness

1 BLESSED (HAPPY, fortunate, prosperous, and enviable) is the man who walks and lives not in the counsel of the ungodly [following their advice, their plans and purposes], nor stands [submissive and inactive] in the path where sinners walk, nor sits down [to relax and rest] where the scornful [and the mockers] gather.

2 But his delight and desire are in the law of the Lord, and on His law (the precepts, the instructions, the teachings of God) he habitually meditates (ponders and studies) by day and by night.

3 And he shall be like a tree firmly planted [and tended] by the streams of water, ready to bring forth its fruit in its season; its leaf also shall not fade or whither; and everything he does shall prosper [and come to maturity].

4 Not so the wicked [those disobedient and living without God are not so]. But they are like the chaff [worthless, dead, without substance] which the wind drives away.

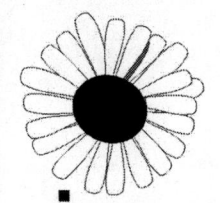

5 Therefore the wicked [those disobedient and living without God] shall not stand [justified] in the judgement, nor sinners in the congregation of the righteous [those who are upright and in right standing with God].

6 For the Lord knows and is fully acquainted with the way of the righteous, but the way of the ungodly [those living outside God's will] shall perish (end in ruin and come to nought).

Psalms 1:1-6(AMP)

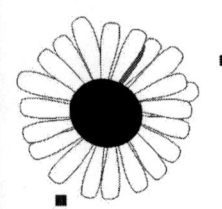

Wisdom

WISDOM: I love those who love me, and those who seek me early and diligently shall find me.

Proverbs 8:17(AMP)

I [Wisdom] walk in the way of righteousness (moral and spiritual rectitude in every area and relation), in the midst of the paths of justice,

Proverbs 8:20(AMP)

Blessed (happy, fortunate, to be envied) is the man who listens to me, watching daily at my gates, waiting at the posts of my doors. For whoever finds me [Wisdom] finds life and draws forth and obtains favor from the Lord.

Proverbs 8:34-35(AMP)

Prize Wisdom highly and exalt her, and she will exalt and promote you; she will bring you to honor when you embrace her.

Proverbs 4 :8 (AMP)

Love,
Wisdom

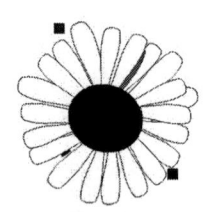

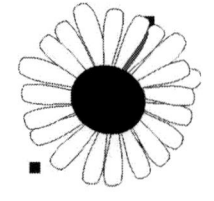

The wise also will hear and increase in learning, and the person of understanding will acquire skill and attain to sound counsel [so that he may be able to steer his course rightly].
                                      Proverbs 1:5 (AMP)

The reverent and worshipful fear of the Lord is the beginning and the principle and choice part of knowledge [its starting point and its essence]; but fools despise skillful and godly Wisdom, instruction and discipline.
                                      Proverbs 1:7 (AMP)

But whoso hearkens to me [Wisdom] shall dwell securely and in confident trust shall be quiet, without fear or dread of evil.
                                      Proverbs 1:33 (AMP)

MY SON, if you will receive my words and treasure up my commandments within you, Making your ear attentive to skillful and godly Wisdom and inclining and directing your heart and mind to understanding [applying all your powers to quest for it]; Yes, if you cry out for insight and raise your voice for understanding, If you seek [Wisdom] as for silver and search for skillful and godly wisdom as for hidden treasures, then you will understand the reverent and worshipful fear of the Lord and find the knowledge of [our omniscient] God.
                                      Proverbs 2:1-5 (AMP)

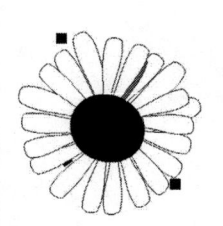

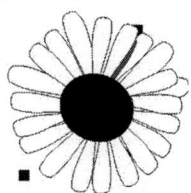

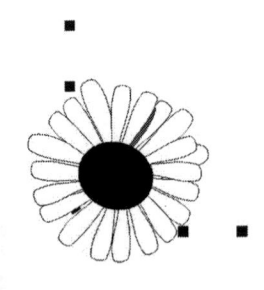

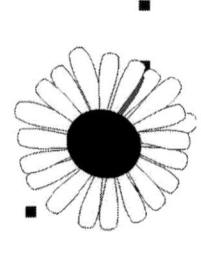

Notes

Part 8

Did You Know?

You Were Created By Design For A Destiny And Purpose . . .

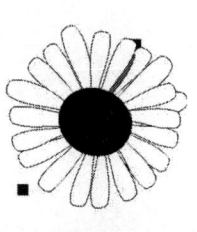

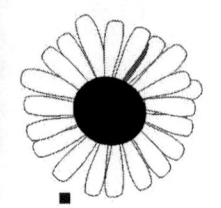

The Origin Of Life—
How You Originated . . .

By Creation: You Are Fearfully and Wonderfully Made!

I will praise thee; for I am fearfully and wonderfully made: marvelous are thy works; and that my soul knoweth right well.
                                              Psalms 139:14(KJV)

Did you Know?
Man was created by God on the sixth day of creation. And God said, Let us make man in our own image, after our likeness: and let them have dominion over the fish of the sea, and over the fowl of the air, and over every creeping thing that creepeth upon the earth. So God created man in his own image, in the image of God created he him: male and female created he them.
                                              Genesis 1:26-27(KJV)

Did You Know?
Man's body was shaped from the dust, but he became a living soul only after God breathed the breath of life in his nostrils.

And the Lord God formed man of the dust of the ground, and breathed into his nostrils the breath of life; and man became a living soul.
                                              Genesis 2:7(KJV)

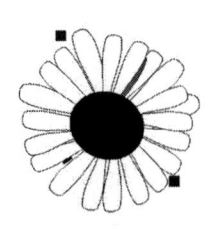

Design of Woman

Did You Know?
Woman was made from the rib (side) of man.

And the Lord God caused a deep sleep to fall upon Adam; and while he slept, He took one of his ribs or a part of his side and closed up the [place with] flesh. And the rib or part of his side which the Lord God had taken from the man He built up and made into a woman, and He brought her to the man.
Genesis 2:21-22(AMP)

Then Adam said. This [creature] is now bone of my bones and flesh of my flesh; she shall be called Woman, because she was taken out of Man.
Genesis 2:23 (AMP)

Common Names Woman is Known By . . .

Females   Ladies   Women

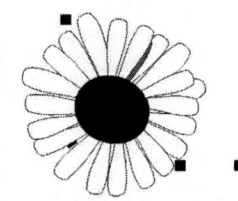

Girls   Daughters

Princess   Queens

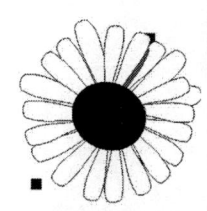

God Created Our Bodies to Live and Walk on Planet Earth

Did you know?
Your unique Body has a Spirit and Soul.

BODY—SPIRIT—SOUL

1. The Spirit is the real person that lives inside the body. Most inner resident—Human spirit

2. The Soul is made up of the will, mind and emotions. The inner man—Your Personality

3. The Body is the house humans live in. Most outer—Your Body-flesh, physical senses for the natural world

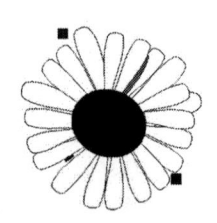

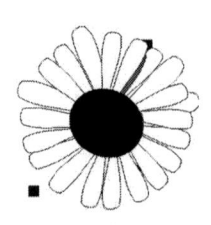

God is Spirit and Spirit forever lives. Therefore God lives inside of us. That is what gives us the life of Christ that dwells within our bodies. We belong to God and He allowed us to be on Earth for His purposes (work).

And I have filled him with the spirit of God, in wisdom, and in understanding, and in knowledge, and in all manner of workmanship, to devise cunning works, to work in gold, and in silver, and in brass, And in cutting the stones, to set them, all manner of workmanship.
Exodus 31:3-5(KJV)

Just as God commanded and chose Bezaleel given to him the skill and ability to design and engage in all kinds of craftsmanship. He has chosen you to fulfill a specific task for a specific time and purpose. As you develop to live life skillfully and produce something of quality unto the Lord, you will know how to work all manner of work for the services of God.

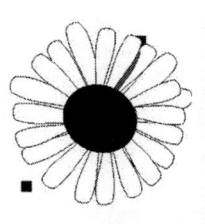

Learning to Understand God's Ownership

Did you know?
You don't own anything—God owns everything. You, other people, possessions, your job, your money, all of your time, and the air you breath—it all belongs to Him.

THE EARTH is the Lord's, and the fullness thereof; the world, and they that dwell therein.
Psalms 24:1 (KJV)

Once you have learned to realize that everything in God's earth is on loan to you. You will become more respectful and appreciative to people by honoring, giving and releasing possessions very freely.

Do you not know that your body is the temple (the very sanctuary) of the Holy Spirit Who lives within you, Whom you have received [as a Gift] from God? You are not your own, You were bought with a price [purchased with a preciousness and paid for, made His own]. So then, honor God and bring glory to Him in your body.
I Corinthians 6:19-20(AMP)

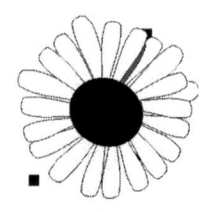

Purpose

Did You Know?
Many people go through life never finding out their God-given purpose, but you don't have to be one of those people. To know your God-given purpose, you must ask God the one who created you.

I [the Lord] will instruct you and teach you in the way you should go; I will counsel you with my eye upon you.
Psalms 32:8 (AMP)

Before you were ever born, God designed a purpose for your life. A purpose that no other human could ever fulfill.

Don't be quick to run to man for the answers; ASK GOD. All instruction is found in the counsel of God.

Give instruction to a wise man and he will be yet wiser; teach a righteous man (one upright and in right standing with God) and he will increase in learning.
Proverbs 9:9 (AMP)

For we are his workmanship, created in Christ Jesus unto good works, which God hath before ordained that we should walk in them.
Ephesians 2:10 (KJV)

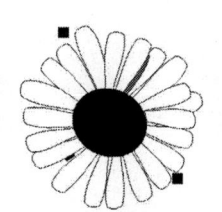

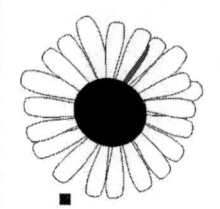

Did You Know?
YOU MUST LEARN HOW TO WALK WITH GOD

Listed are a few things that will prepare you as you learn how to walk with God:

- You must be born again (birthed of the Spirit) become a new creature, by accepting the Lord Jesus Christ as your personal Saviour.

Jesus answered and said unto him, Verily, verily, I say unto thee, Except a man be born again, he cannot see the kingdom of God. Nicodemus said unto him, How can a man be born when he is old? Can he enter the second time into his mother's womb, and be born? Jesus answered, Verily, verily, I say unto thee, Except a man be born of water and of the Spirit, he cannot enter into the kingdom of God.
John 3:3-5(KJV)

For the kingdom of God is not meat and drink; but righteousness, and peace, and joy in the Holy Ghost.
Romans 14:17(KJV)

- You must faithfully attend a bible believing church as often as you can.
- You must pray and meditate on God's word every day. But his delight is in the law of the Lord; and in his law doth he meditate day and night. Psalms 1:2(KJV)

- You must spend quality time in the presence of God, in prayer, praise and worship.
- You must seek God for revelation and clarity of what His plan is for your life.
- You must fast and pray
- You must obey God

But without faith it is impossible to please and be satisfactory to Him. For whoever would come near to God must [necessarily] believe that God exists and that He is the rewarder of those who earnestly and diligently seek Him (out).

Hebrews 11:6(AMP)

Did You Know?

There is a greatness on the inside of you

Discover your greatness by diligently seeking the one who knows everything about you.

GOD—THE CREATOR AND RULER OF THE UNIVERSE

Proving Yourself

Q. Can you pass your test?
A. Yes.

Q. Can you prove you're committed to God?
A. Yes, through your actions. You are committed to righteousness and your God-given destiny.

Q. Are you more knowledgeable?
A. Yes, you have acquired more wisdom, knowledge and understanding of your physical body and your spirit man.

FACING THE CHALLENGE

Now that you have wisdom, knowledge, and understanding, take the challenge and apply what you've learned in your daily life.

Give instruction to a wise man and he will be yet wiser; teach a righteous man (one upright and in right standing with God) and he will increase in learning. The reverent and worshipful fear of the Lord is the beginning (the chief and choice part) of Wisdom, and the knowledge of the Holy One is insight and understanding. For by me [Wisdom from God] your days shall be multiplied, and the years of your life shall be increased.
Proverbs 9:9-11 (AMP)

GOD IS LOVE

For God so greatly loved and dearly prized the world that He [even] gave up His only begotten (unique) Son, so that whoever believes in (trusts in, clings to, relies on) Him shall not perish (come to destruction, be lost) but have eternal (everlasting) life.
John 3:16(AMP)

And may the God of peace Himself sanctify you through and through [separate you from profane things, make you pure and wholly consecrated to God]; and may your spirit and soul and body be preserved sound and complete [and found] blameless at the coming of our Lord Jesus Christ (the Messiah).
I Thessalonians 5:23(AMP)

Beloved, let us love one another: for love is of God; and every one that loveth is born of God, and knoweth God.
I John 4:7(KJV)

No man hath seen God at any time. If we love one another, God dwelleth in us, and his love perfected in us.
1 John 4:12 (KJV)

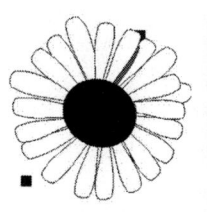

KNOW THAT GOD IS PERFECT IN POWER, WISDOM, and GOODNESS!

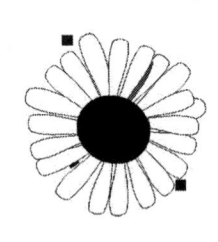

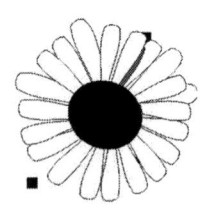

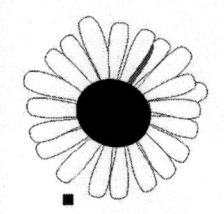

References

American College of Obstetricians and Gynecologist. "Your First Ob-Gyn Visit."
ACOG 2001. Patient Education Pamphlet AP 150. Washington, DC:

The Encyclopedic Atlas of the Human Body. Global Book Publishing 2004. A Visual Guide To The Human Body 2004. Global Book Publishing.

The American Heritage Dictionary. 2006. Houghton Mifflin Company

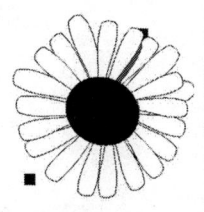

Conclusion

No matter how old you are, listen attentively to what God is saying to you. You must obey and humble yourselves as little children. Stay in tune with your spirit and patiently wait for instruction from God.

Truly I tell you, whoever does not receive and accept and welcome the kingdom of God like a little child [does] positively shall not enter it at all. And He took them [the children up one by one] in His arms and [fervently invoked a] blessing, placing His hands upon them.

Mark 10:15-16(AMP)

Today is a new day! Gone are the days of not knowing. As you flipped through the pages of this book, it is my hope and prayer that you are educated and inspired to practice living your life to the fullest. Although challenges will come, know that you are never alone, God is always by your side.

When you pass through the waters, I will be with you, and through the rivers, they will not overwhelm you. When you walk through the fire, you will not be burned or scorched, nor will the flame kindle upon you.

Isaiah 43:2 (AMP)

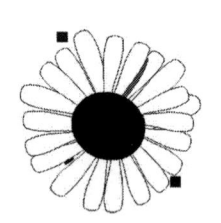

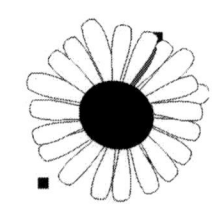

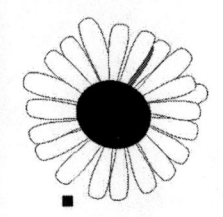

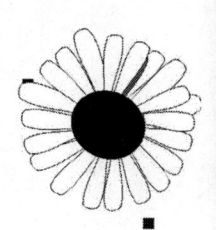

About the Author

Rebecca Baker is a native Detroiter, faithful wife, mother of four daughters and grandmother of five. Life as a youth brought many challenges for her; from low self—esteem to growing up too fast. Thankfully God brought her through with His grace and mercy. Despite her past experiences, she desired to have a closer relationship with God; learning who she is as a person and developing a higher self esteem.

Rebecca faithfully serves in the choir and intercessory prayer engine ministries at Detroit World Outreach Church in Redford, Michigan. She now understands that every negative experience she had is for a Holy reason. In order for God to get her to destiny, she had to go through some things. Now she can share her testimony and bless young girls who are in the same position she was in. Baker shares useful information that many girls should know, but they don't. She knows firsthand how the stages of puberty can affect a young girl's life. Baker has successfully equipped her four daughters with the information they needed to embrace their transition into womanhood.

During her life as a young girl, as her body began to develop, it was one of the scariest moments of her life.

Baker has priceless knowledge obtained by her own personal experiences while raising her four daughters. Over the years she has developed patience and wisdom through the grace of God.

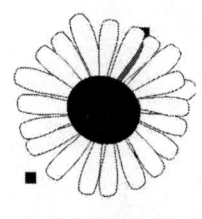

Calling All Girls CREED

We accept the fact we can't change our body design: size, height, skin color, or hair. Our beauty is within.

We are unique, one of a kind; capable of excelling in all that we do. Our brilliant minds are always ready to handle challenges.

We are confident in our decision making, hearts full of love, able to forgive, forget, and have respect for others as well as ourselves.

We represent holiness in right standing with God. Standing Tall Not to Fall to the Things of the WORLD!!!

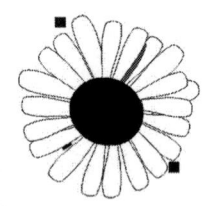

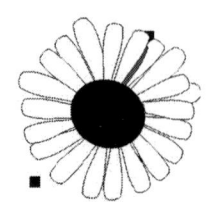

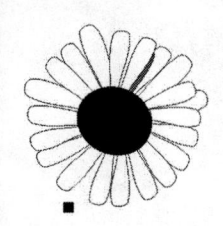

GOD IS CALLING ALL OF HIS CHILDREN TO BE SAVED

Being saved, requires you to take the first step, by confessing with your mouth, the Prayer of Salvation to accept Jesus Christ as your personal Saviour. Making Him Lord of your life. Salvation is a free gift from God to those who believe.

Being saved is as simple as praying the prayer below.

Heavenly Father, I come to you in the name of Jesus: Your word says, whosoever shall call on the name of the Lord shall be saved (Acts 2:21). I'm calling on You. I pray and ask Jesus to come into my heart and be Lord over my Life. According to (Romans 10: 9-10) "If thou shalt confess with thy mouth the Lord Jesus, and shalt **Believe** in thine heart that God hath raised him from the dead, thou shalt be saved. For with the heart man believeth unto righteousness; and with the mouth confession is made unto salvation. I confess with my mouth and **Believe** in my heart that God raised Jesus from the dead, and that my sins are forgiven.

HE IS LORD! AMEN I am Saved! A Born Again Believer!

Now refer to pages 98 & 99 to learn how to walk with God.